BIBLE NEWS PROPHECY

 8

 16

 31

In This Issue:

2 **From the Editor: 25 Reasons Not to Celebrate Christmas** Early Christians did not celebrate Christmas. Should you?

4 **Gaza and the Palestinians** Does the Bible have prophecies related to the Palestinians or those of Gaza?

8 **The Fifth Commandment** Do you honor your father and mother? Are you an honourable parent?

16 **Study the Bible Course Lesson 16b: You Must Be Born Again!**

27 **Happiness Is …** Is happiness wealth and power? What can bring happiness to humankind?

31 **Youth and Singles Q&A** This article answers questions some teens and singles have wondered about.

Back Cover: Internet and Radio This shows where people can find the messages from the *Continuing* Church of God.

About the Front Cover: While Gaza City can give the impression of being like others around the world, Gaza is quite different. Cover developed for the *Continuing* Church of God.

Bible News Prophecy magazine is published by the *Continuing* Church of God, 1036 W. Grand Avenue, Grover Beach, CA, 93433. http://www.ccog.org

©2019 *Continuing* Church of God. Printed in the U.S.A. All rights reserved.

Reproduction in whole or in part without written permission is prohibited. We do respect your privacy and we do not rent, trade, or sell our mailing list. If you do not want to receive this magazine, simply contact our Grover Beach office. Scripture references are from the New King James Version (©Thomas Nelson, Inc., Publishers, used by permission or for 20th century articles the KJV) unless otherwise noted.

Bible News Prophecy – SUPPORTED BY YOUR CONTRIBUTIONS

Bible News Prophecy has no subscription or newsstand price. This magazine is provided free of charge by the Continuing Church of God. It is made possible by the voluntary, freely given tithes and offerings of the membership of the Church and others who have elected to support the work of the Church. Contributions are gratefully welcomed and are tax-deductible in the U.S. Those who wish to voluntarily aid and support this worldwide Work of God are gladly welcomed as co-workers in this major effort to preach and publish the gospel to all nations. Contributions should be sent to: Continuing Church of God, 1036 W. Grand Avenue, Grover Beach, CA, 93433.

Editor in Chief: Bob Thiel

Copy/Proofing Editor: Joyce Thiel

Proofreader: John Hickey;
SBC Course Assister: Shirley Gestro.

Photos: All photos come from the Thiel family or public domain sources such as Wikipedia, Pixabay, or certain governments (unless specific attribution is given).

Layout and Design:
James Erwin Estoque

October – December 2019

FROM THE EDITOR IN CHIEF: BOB THIEL

25 Things to Consider About Christmas

Many who claim Christianity celebrate December 25th as the date of Jesus' birth.

Yet, many do not understand the biblical or historical truth about it.

Here is a list of 25 items people who keep Christmas seem not to fully consider:

1. In Leviticus 23, God lists His festivals—with specific dates.

2. In Jeremiah 10, God says not to follow pagan practices, such as using a decorated tree, in the worship of Him.

3. Nowhere in the Bible is the date of Jesus' birth mentioned.

4. Scripture opposes the view that Jesus could have been born in late December because the "census would have been impossible in winter" per The Catholic Encyclopedia and because shepherds were not spending the night outside with their flocks then.

5. Nowhere in the Bible is anyone instructed to observe the date of Jesus' birth.

6. The Bible does not show that Jesus' disciples ever observed the date of Jesus' birth.

7. At the time of Christ, observant Jews did not celebrate birthdays, nor did early Christians.

8. The Apostle Paul wrote that Christians were not to use demonic pagan practices (1 Corinthians 10:20).

9. Christmas was NOT part of the "faith once for all delivered to the saints" (Jude 3).

10. Early church writings do not show that any Christian observed the date of Jesus' birth.

11. The sun god Mithras was allegedly born on December 25th as the season was celebrated as the rebirth of the sun.

12. Pagans celebrated the sun-god Mithras and the god of agriculture Saturn in late December each year with lights, wreaths, parties, and gift-giving.

13. About 2 centuries after Jesus was born, Tertullian wrote that people in what we would now call the Eastern and Roman Catholic churches, used wreaths and lights, gave gifts, etc. in late December to be like the heathen. Pagan worship really is the "reason for the season".

14. Tertullian condemned those practices as demonic and idolatrous and further wrote that those who professed Christ should not honor pagan gods in their worship.

15. The pagan Emperor Constantine worshiped the sun-god Mithras and celebrated Jesus' birth on December 25th starting in 336 A.D.

16. Roman pontiffs followed Emperor Constantine's lead and in 354 A.D., Bishop Liberius of Rome ordered the people to celebrate on December 25.

17. The anti-Semite Constantinople Bishop John Chrysostom, who opposed the biblical holy days, got a December 25th celebration adopted in his area by 395 A.D.

18. The word for Christmas in late Old English is Cristes Maesse, the Mass of Christ, first found in 1038, and Cristes-messe, in 1131. It most certainly did not come from the Bible.

19. The "twelve days of Christmas" originally came from the 12 days of Yuletide which began at sunset on December 20, known as Mother Night, and ended on the night of December 31, the Night of the Oak King and the Roman day of Hecate.

20. Mistletoe came from the pagan Druids.

21. Yule logs were originally a scandal to the Church of Rome, but were later embraced.

22. Roman Catholics originally condemned Protestantism as the "Tannenbaum religion" because of what are called Christmas trees. But now Vatican City prominently displays one each year.

23. It is wrong to bear false witness, including telling lies about the mythological Santa Claus.

24. Christmas is NOT a biblical nor truly a Christ-centered holiday. It is a sentimental and commercialized pagan tradition.

25. The Apostle Paul warned Christians that they were not above God's wrath for combining pagan traditions with Christian practices (1 Corinthians 10:21).

Christmas is a distraction from the Gospel of the Kingdom of God. It is not a truly Christ-centered holiday as its proponents sometimes claim.

Christmas has the wrong emphasis and is not based on truth.

Jesus taught:

> 24 God is Spirit, and those who worship Him must worship in spirit and truth. (John 4:24)
>
> 7 And in vain they worship Me, Teaching as doctrines the commandments of men.' (Mark 7:7)

There is a right way and a wrong way to live and worship God—do not base this on your emotional feelings about what is right:

> 8 You shall not at all do as we are doing here today—every man doing whatever is right in his own eyes— ... 25 do what is right in the sight of the Lord. ... 32 Whatever I command you, be careful to observe it; you shall not add to it nor take away from it. (Deuteronomy 12:8,25,32)

God did not command keeping Christmas: pagans came up with it.

Consider also what the Apostle Paul wrote:

> 21 You cannot drink the cup of the Lord and the cup of demons; you cannot partake of the Lord's table and of the table of demons. 22 Or do we provoke the Lord to jealousy? Are we stronger than He? (1 Corinthians 10:21-22)
>
> 17 This I say, therefore, and testify in the Lord, that you should no longer walk as the rest of the Gentiles walk, in the futility of their mind, 18 having their understanding darkened, being alienated from the life of God, because of the ignorance that is in them, because of the blindness of their heart; 19 who, being past feeling, have given themselves over to lewdness, to work all uncleanness with greediness.
>
> 20 But you have not so learned Christ, 21 if indeed you have heard Him and have been taught by Him, as the truth is in Jesus: 22 that you put off, concerning your former conduct, the old man which grows corrupt according to the deceitful lusts, 23 and be renewed in the spirit of your mind, 24 and that you put on the new man which was created according to God, in true righteousness and holiness. (Ephesians 4:17-24)

Christians are to put off pagan ways, and live according to the truth, not longing for improper traditions.

Wiccans' (witches) still keep Yule and teach the altar on Yule should face north and that the area is decorated with Holly and Mistletoe. They think that is good.

The foundation of Christmas is demonic paganism and lies—it is not biblical.

Consider something else that Jesus had recorded:

> 14 Blessed are those who do His commandments, that they may have the right to the tree of life, and may enter through the gates into the city. 15 But outside are dogs and sorcerers and sexually immoral and murderers and idolaters, and whoever loves and practices a lie. (Revelation 22:14-15)

Which are you?

One who keeps God's commandments or one who prefers to practice the idolatrous lie of Christmas?

To learn more about biblical holy days and various holidays, check out the free online booklet: 'Should You Keep God's Holy Days or Demonic Holidays?' Available at www.ccog.org.

Gaza and the Palestinians in Bible Prophecy

City of Gaza

By Bob Thiel

The Palestinian-dominated areas of the West Bank and Gaza have been in the news a lot. A violence-prone group known as Hamas essentially runs the region called Gaza.

What will happen to Gaza? Does the Bible teach anything about the Palestinians?

Does the Bible have anything to say about Gaza and/or the Palestinians?

Gaza, itself, is mentioned in both the Old and New Testaments. And some of those mentions involve statements that are prophetic.

Gaza, `Azzah (az-zaw'), is the feminine form of the Hebrew word 'az that means strong, vehement, or harsh (Biblesoft's New Exhaustive Strong's Numbers and Concordance with Expanded Greek-Hebrew Dictionary. Copyright © 1994, 2003, 2006 Biblesoft, Inc. and International Bible Translators, Inc.).

Where is Gaza? What about Palestine?

Here is some information about Gaza:

The Gaza Strip (/ˈɡɑːzəˈstrɪp/; Arabic: قطاع غزة‎ Qiṭāʿ Ġazzah [qɪˈtˤɑːʕ ˈɣazza]), or simply Gaza, is a Palestinian region on the eastern coast of the Mediterranean Sea that borders Egypt on the southwest for 11 kilometers (6.8 mi) and Israel on the east and north along a 51 km (32 mi) border.

In 1994, Israel granted the right of self-governance to Gaza through the Palestinian Authority. Prior to this, Gaza had been subject to military occupation, most recently by Israel (1967–94) and by Egypt (1958–67), and earlier by Syria when Gaza had been part of the Ottoman Empire. Since 2007, the Gaza Strip has been de-facto governed by Hamas, a Palestinian group claiming to be the representatives of the Palestinian National Authority and the Palestinian people. In 2012, the United Nations General Assembly "accorded Palestine non-Member Observer State status in the

United Nations". Gaza forms a part of the Palestinian territory defined in the Oslo Agreements and UNSC Resolution 1860. (Gaza, Wikipedia, viewed 07/26/14)

Basically, the nation calling itself Israel took Gaza in the 1967 war. Later, Israel turned Gaza over to the Palestinian Authority to govern, though Israel, technically considers it part of its territory. Most in Gaza are Palestinian Muslims who do not wish to be part of Israel. Around two million Palestinians live in neighboring Jordan.

According to the commentary at Nelson's Study Bible Gaza, Ashkelon, Ashdod and Ekron were the major cities of the Philistines and that the term Cherethites is simply another name for Philistines. Those cities/regions are currently primarily occupied by the Palestinians.

Notice what the Bible says about the origin of the Philistines:

> 6 The sons of Ham were Cush, Mizraim, Put, and Canaan. (Genesis 10:6)
>
> 13 Mizraim begot Ludim, Anamim, Lehabim, Naphtuhim, 14 Pathrusim, and Casluhim (from whom came the Philistines and Caphtorim). (Genesis 10:13-14)

Basically the Palestinians seem to have come from descendants of Casluhim (Genesis 10:14) who likely mixed with descendants of Ishmael (cf. Genesis 16:10-12).

Notice also the following from the old Radio Church of God:

Where Are the Canaanites Today?

Originally the sons of Canaan settled in Palestine. Canaan, remember, was the first born of Ham. Canaan's descendants — and this includes the other sons of Ham — were to be "servant of servants" (Gen.9:25). Their children are to serve both Shem and Japheth (verses 26,27). There is nothing wrong with serving — we all have to learn to serve. Shem and Japheth must become God's servants, too. That is why Canaan is called a "servant of servants."

Many have quoted this in direct reference to the Negro. As brothers of Canaan, the Negroes have shared the same position in life, but Negroes are not Canaanites.

The Canaanites were great traffickers of old. The word Canaanite in Zech.14:21 is, in fact, translated as "trafficker" in the Jewish translation. The Sidonians, descendants of Canaan, were famous seamen in the days of Solomon. The Greeks called them "Phoenicians". But the Phoenicians called themselves "Kna" or "Knana", meaning Canaanite. (See SMITH'S BIBLE DICTIONARY).

When Israel entered the land of Palestine under Joshua, whole tribes of the Canaanites were destroyed or driven out of central Palestine (Judges 3:1-4) because some of the Canaanites were extremely degenerate in their morals.

Now turn to Gen. 10:18, "Afterward were the families of the Canaanites spread abroad". Where did they journey?

The Canaanites settled the island of Malta and parts of Sicily, Southern Italy, Sardinia, North Africa and even Southern Spain and Portugal, where the sons of Javan were already living. (See ENCY. BRIT., articles, "Malta", "Sicily", "Carthage", etc. Most people are familiar with the Phoenicians from grade and high school days. In North Africa the Canaanites are called Moors — -a name probably derived from Amors, the Hebrew form of "Amorites".

From these lands they have spread into North and South America since the days of Columbus. The Portuguese — of mixed Canaanite and Tarshish stock — have settled much of Brazil. And the Sicilians are thick in big cities in America. The underworld "Mafia" organization which springs from Canaanitish Sicily, is but a modern version of their ancient tendency to traffic among the nations of the world.

Canaanites have also intermarried into Esau — Turkey today (Gen.26:34), and Judah (Gen.38:2), and Israel (Judges 3:5-7).

Only a few Canaanites remain in North Palestine and Lebanon. The Canaanites are seldom included in the prophecies which pertain to this twentieth century. They exert no great position or influence in the world.

The main body of non-Jewish inhabitants of Palestine today are not Canaanites, but Philistines!

Who Are the Philistines?

The Philistines are first mentioned in Genesis 10:14. They are a branch of the Mizraim, from Ham.

Mizraim is commonly applied to Egypt. In fact, "Mizr" is the name which the natives still apply to Egypt today. The Greeks called the land Aegyptus — hence our Egypt. Josephus said that not all the people from Mizraim inhabited Africa.

But not all of Mizraim live in Egypt today!

Where did the children of Mizraim settle?

First, notice that the Mizraim first settled on the northeast corner of the Mediterranean Sea.

From there they spread through the Eastern Mediterranean isles and into Africa (ENCYCLOPAEDIA BIBLICA, "Mizraim").

The Philistines, who came from Mizraim, inhabited Southern Palestine even in the days of Abraham (Gen.21:34). They are still there today — in the Gaza strip in Palestine — causing no end of trouble (Zech.9:6-7). The Philistines (a branch of the family of Casluhim) settled originally on the Island of Crete in the Mediterranean. Crete is called, in the Bible, Caphtor (Jer.47:4 and Amos 9:7). The Island of Caphtor was originally settled by the Caphtorim, a tribe of Mizraim (Gen.10:14). Both the Philistines and the Caphtorim destroyed the Canaanites in South Palestine and lived in their place (Deut.2:23). No wonder there are so few Canaanites left! (Hoeh H. The TRUTH about the RACE QUESTION! Plain Truth, July 1957)

As far as the word Palestine goes, notice also the following:

> Though the definite origins of the word "Palestine" have been debated for years and are still not known for sure, the name is believed to be derived from the Egyptian and Hebrew word peleshet. Roughly translated to mean "rolling" or "migratory," the term was used to describe the inhabitants of the land to the northeast of Egypt - the Philistines. The Philistines were an Aegean people - more closely related to the Greeks and with no connection ethnically, linguisticly or historically with Arabia - who conquered in the 12th Century BCE the Mediterranean coastal plain that is now Israel and Gaza.
>
> A derivative of the name "Palestine" first appears in Greek literature in the 5th Century BCE when the historian Herodotus called the area "Palaistinē" (Greek - Παλαιστίνη). In the 2nd century CE, the Romans crushed the revolt of Shimon Bar Kokhba (132 CE), during which Jerusalem and Judea were regained and the area of Judea was renamed Palaestina in an attempt to minimize Jewish identification with the land of Israel. (Origins of the Name "Palestine". viewed 07/26/14)

The term Philistines in the Bible refers to people who tended to occupy regions including Gaza. The NKJV uses the term Philistines 252 times and the term Philistine 34 times.

The Bible Tells of Gaza

The NKJV has the term "Gaza" 21 times and "Gazites" twice.

Here is the first time Gaza is mentioned in the Bible:

> 15 Canaan begot Sidon his firstborn, and Heth; 16 the Jebusite, the Amorite, and the Girgashite; 17 the Hivite, the Arkite, and the Sinite; 18 the Arvadite, the Zemarite, and the Hamathite. Afterward the families of the Canaanites were dispersed. 19 And the border of the Canaanites was from Sidon as you go toward Gerar, as far as Gaza; then as you go toward Sodom, Gomorrah, Admah, and Zeboiim, as far as Lasha. 20 These were the sons of Ham, according to their families, according to their languages, in their lands and in their nations. (Genesis 10:15-20)

The first biblically mentioned inhabitants of Gaza were Canaanites that descended from Noah's son Ham. But as it was a border region, over time, the ethnic character apparently became mixed. And there were changes:

> 20 (That was also regarded as a land of giants; giants formerly dwelt there. But the Ammonites call them Zamzummim, 21 a people as great

and numerous and tall as the Anakim. But the Lord destroyed them before them, and they dispossessed them and dwelt in their place, 22 just as He had done for the descendants of Esau, who dwelt in Seir, when He destroyed the Horites from before them. They dispossessed them and dwelt in their place, even to this day. 23 And the Avim, who dwelt in villages as far as Gaza — the Caphtorim, who came from Caphtor, destroyed them and dwelt in their place.) (Deuteronomy 2:20-23)

The Bible shows that Joshua later conquered areas in that region:

> 41 And Joshua conquered them from Kadesh Barnea as far as Gaza, and all the country of Goshen, even as far as Gibeon. (Joshua 10:41)

> 22 None of the Anakim were left in the land of the children of Israel; they remained only in Gaza, in Gath, and in Ashdod. (Joshua 11:22)

> 21 The cities at the limits of the tribe of the children of Judah...33 In the lowland:... 47 Ashdod with its towns and villages, Gaza with its towns and villages — as far as the Brook of Egypt and the Great Sea with its coastline. (Joshua 15:21, 33, 47)

> 1 Now Joshua was old, advanced in years. And the Lord said to him: "You are old, advanced in years, and there remains very much land yet to be possessed. 2 This is the land that yet remains: all the territory of the Philistines and all that of the Geshurites, 3 from Sihor, which is east of Egypt, as far as the border of Ekron northward (which is counted as Canaanite); the five lords of the Philistines — the Gazites, the Ashdodites, the Ashkelonites, the Gittites, and the Ekronites; also the Avites (Joshua 13:1-3).

The time also came when Gaza was conquered to become part of the Israeli territory of Judah:

> 18 Also Judah took Gaza with its territory, Ashkelon with its territory, and Ekron with its territory. 19 So the Lord was with Judah. And they drove out the mountaineers, but they could not drive out the inhabitants of the lowland, because they had chariots of iron. (Judges 1:18-19)

But the situation changed:

> 1 Then the children of Israel did evil in the sight of the Lord. So the Lord delivered them into the hand of Midian for seven years, 2 and the hand of Midian prevailed against Israel. Because of the Midianites, the children of Israel made for themselves the dens, the caves, and the strongholds which are in the mountains. 3 So it was, whenever Israel had sown, Midianites would come up; also Amalekites and the people of the East would come up against them. 4 Then they would encamp against them and destroy the produce of the earth as far as Gaza, and leave no sustenance for Israel, neither sheep nor ox nor donkey. (Judges 6:1-4)

Samson had interest in a Gentile in Gaza and once had to escape from the city of Gaza:

> 1 Now Samson went to Gaza and saw a harlot there, and went in to her. 2 When the Gazites were told, "Samson has come here!" they surrounded the place and lay in wait for him all night at the gate of the city. They were quiet all night, saying, "In the morning, when it is daylight, we will kill him." 3 And Samson lay low till midnight; then he arose at midnight, took hold of the doors of the gate of the city and the two gateposts, pulled them up, bar and all, put them on his shoulders, and carried them to the top of the hill that faces Hebron. (Judges 16:1-3)

Later, after he was betrayed by Delilah, Samson was brought to Gaza where his eyes were removed:

> 18 When Delilah saw that he had told her all his heart, she sent and called for the lords of the Philistines, saying, "Come up once more, for he has told me all his heart." So the lords of the Philistines came up to her and brought the money in their hand. 19 Then she lulled him to sleep on her knees, and called for a man and had him shave off the seven locks of his head. Then she began to torment him, and his strength left him. 20 And she said, "The Philistines are upon you, Samson!" So he awoke from his sleep, and said, "I will go out as before, at other times, and shake myself free!" But he did not know that the Lord had departed from him.

> 21 Then the Philistines took him and put out his eyes, and brought him down to Gaza. They

bound him with bronze fetters, and he became a grinder in the prison. 22 However, the hair of his head began to grow again after it had been shaven. (Judges 16:18-22)

Samson was brought out of that prison to the temple of Dagon during a sacrifice to Dagon. There he asked to be put between the two pillars that held up that temple, pushed them down, and died with the Philistines (Judges 16:25-30). It was apparently close to the prison, and hence Samson seemingly died in Gaza.

After they attained, then returned the Ark of the Covenant to the children of Israel, the Philistines offered something for each of their five main cities/regions, one of which was Gaza:

> 17 These are the golden tumors which the Philistines returned as a trespass offering to the Lord: one for Ashdod, one for Gaza, one for Ashkelon, one for Gath, one for Ekron; 18 and the golden rats, according to the number of all the cities of the Philistines belonging to the five lords, both fortified cities and country villages (1 Samuel 6:17-18)

Solomon, who was of the tribe of Judah, extended the reign of Israel to Gaza:

> 22 Now Solomon's provision for one day was thirty kors of fine flour, sixty kors of meal, 23 ten fatted oxen, twenty oxen from the pastures, and one hundred sheep, besides deer, gazelles, roebucks, and fatted fowl.
>
> 24 For he had dominion over all the region on this side of the River from Tiphsah even to Gaza, namely over all the kings on this side of the River; and he had peace on every side all around him. (1 Kings 4:22-24)

After some territory was lost, Hezekiah, the king of Judah extended his reign to Gaza:

> 1 Now it came to pass in the third year of Hoshea the son of Elah, king of Israel, that Hezekiah the son of Ahaz, king of Judah, began to reign… 7 The Lord was with him; he prospered wherever he went. And he rebelled against the king of Assyria and did not serve him. 8 He subdued the Philistines, as far as Gaza and its territory, from watchtower to fortified city. (2 Kings 18:1,7-8)

Thus, history indicates that the Philistines would gain and lose territory near Gaza, as did the Israelites, although this seems to show that it was mainly dominated by the Philistines.

The New Testament mentions Gaza:

> 26 Now an angel of the Lord spoke to Philip, saying, "Arise and go toward the south along the road which goes down from Jerusalem to Gaza." This is desert. (Acts 8:26)

On this road Philip met the "Ethiopian eunuch" and after speaking with him, baptized him.

Bible Prophecy Tells About Gaza and Palestine

Zechariah had a prophecy of change coming to Gaza:

> 5 Ashkelon shall see it and fear; Gaza also shall be very sorrowful; And Ekron, for He dried up her expectation. The king shall perish from Gaza, And Ashkelon shall not be inhabited. 6 "A mixed race shall settle in Ashdod, And I will cut off the pride of the Philistines. 7 I will take away the blood from his mouth, And the abominations from between his teeth. But he who remains, even he shall be for our God, And shall be like a leader in Judah, And Ekron like a Jebusite. 8 I will camp around My house Because of the army, Because of him who passes by and him who returns. No more shall an oppressor pass through them, For now I have seen with My eyes. (Zechariah 9:5-8)

Some (see Matthew Henry's Commentary, etc.) believe that this was fulfilled in the past. However, as future prophecies tell of a time of Gaza and the Philistines having problems (see below), the above could still have future fulfillment. If so, it shows that some in Gaza/Palestine will be converted.

Bible prophecy tells of calamity coming to Gaza and other lands:

> 17 Then I took the cup from the Lord's hand, and made all the nations drink, to whom the Lord had sent me: 18 Jerusalem and the cities of Judah, its kings and its princes, to make them a desolation, an astonishment, a hissing, and a curse, as it is this day; 19 Pharaoh king of Egypt, his servants, his princes, and all his people; 20

all the mixed multitude, all the kings of the land of Uz, all the kings of the land of the Philistines (namely, Ashkelon, Gaza, Ekron, and the remnant of Ashdod); 21 Edom, Moab, and the people of Ammon; 22 all the kings of Tyre, all the kings of Sidon, and the kings of the coastlands which are across the sea; 23 Dedan, Tema, Buz, and all who are in the farthest corners; 24 all the kings of Arabia and all the kings of the mixed multitude who dwell in the desert; 25 all the kings of Zimri, all the kings of Elam, and all the kings of the Medes; 26 all the kings of the north, far and near, one with another; and all the kingdoms of the world which are on the face of the earth. Also the king of Sheshach shall drink after them.

27 "Therefore you shall say to them, 'Thus says the Lord of hosts, the God of Israel: "Drink, be drunk, and vomit! Fall and rise no more, because of the sword which I will send among you."' 28 And it shall be, if they refuse to take the cup from your hand to drink, then you shall say to them, 'Thus says the Lord of hosts: "You shall certainly drink! 29 For behold, I begin to bring calamity on the city which is called by My name, and should you be utterly unpunished? You shall not be unpunished, for I will call for a sword on all the inhabitants of the earth," says the Lord of hosts.' (Jeremiah 25:17-29)

Many of the lands above are listed as supporters of the final King of the South (Daniel 11:40-43) and/or part of a confederation that will be destroyed that will involve Egypt (Ezekiel 30:3-8).

Some of those lands, Ashkelon (located 50 kilometres south of Tel Aviv, and 13 kilometres north of the border with the Gaza Strip), Ekron (modern Tel Miqne, which is 35 kilometers west of Jerusalem), and Ashdod (located 32 kilometres south of Tel Aviv, 20 km north of Ashkelon, and 53 km west of Jerusalem), are currently dominated by the nation of Israel.

Ashkelon, Tel Migne, and Ashdod are claimed to be part of Israel. They are not in the Gaza Strip (they are all north of it) nor part of the other Palestinian controlled region known as the West Bank. Therefore, it looks like the Palestinians will either control those cities again or be so numerous in it that they are the ones affected in Jeremiah 25. It is my current view that the Palestinians will gain land that the nation of Israel thinks it will continue to control. Since these are not lands currently considered to be ceded in a peace deal, this looks like losses from the State of Israel after the deal of Daniel 9:27 is broken (cf. Daniel 11:31).

The entire 47th chapter of Jeremiah is a prophecy about the Philistines, including Gaza:

1 The word of the Lord that came to Jeremiah the prophet against the Philistines, before Pharaoh attacked Gaza.

2 Thus says the Lord: "Behold, waters rise out of the north, And shall be an overflowing flood; They shall overflow the land and all that is in it, The city and those who dwell within; Then the men shall cry, And all the inhabitants of the land shall wail. 3 At the noise of the stamping hooves of his strong horses, At the rushing of his chariots, At the rumbling of his wheels, The fathers will not look back for their children, Lacking courage, 4 Because of the day that comes to plunder all the Philistines,To cut off from Tyre and Sidon every helper who remains; For the Lord shall plunder the Philistines, The remnant of the country of Caphtor. 5 Baldness has come upon Gaza, Ashkelon is cut off With the remnant of their valley. How long will you cut yourself? 6 "O you sword of the Lord, How long until you are quiet? Put yourself up into your scabbard, Rest and be still! 7 How can it be quiet, Seeing the Lord has given it a charge Against Ashkelon and against the seashore? There He has appointed it." (Jeremiah 47:1-7)

Problems were thus prophesied for Gaza--since there is a duality to some prophecies (e.g. Malachi 4:5 & Matthew 17:10-13), this prophecy Jeremiah recorded may also have future application. This prophecy also suggests that Israel will no longer control Ashkelon.

Amos specifically recorded a prophecy about Gaza:

6 Thus says the Lord:

"For three transgressions of Gaza, and for four, I will not turn away its punishment, Because they took captive the whole captivity To deliver them up to Edom.

7 But I will send a fire upon the wall of Gaza, Which shall devour its palaces.

8 I will cut off the inhabitant from Ashdod, And the one who holds the scepter from Ashkelon; I will turn My hand against Ekron, And the remnant of the Philistines shall perish," Says the Lord God. (Amos 1:6-8)

Ezekiel had a prophecy against Edom (mentioned also above) and then the following about the Philistines:

15 'Thus says the Lord God: "Because the Philistines dealt vengefully and took vengeance with a spiteful heart, to destroy because of the old hatred," 16 therefore thus says the Lord God: "I will stretch out My hand against the Philistines, and I will cut off the Cherethites and destroy the remnant of the seacoast. 17 I will execute great vengeance on them with furious rebukes; and they shall know that I am the Lord, when I lay My vengeance upon them." (Ezekiel 25:15-17)

The Bible is clear that vengeance belongs to God (Romans 12:9; Hebrews 10:30). Apparently (along with the Edomites, Ezekiel 25:15-17, Joel 3:19, Obadiah 8-11, and Psalms 137:7-9), the Palestinians are subject to judgment in the future for their vengeance. Zechariah 9:6 tells of punishment for their pride.

Isaiah seems to speak of this as well:

14 But they shall fly down upon the shoulder of the Philistines toward the west;

Together they shall plunder the people of the East; They shall lay their hand on Edom and Moab; And the people of Ammon shall obey them. 15 The Lord will utterly destroy the tongue of the Sea of Egypt; With His mighty wind He will shake His fist over the River, And strike it in the seven streams, And make men cross over dryshod. (Isaiah 11:14-15)

This seems to include not only those in Gaza, but possibly those in the West Bank ("the people of the East") and beyond.

Also notice what Zephaniah prophesied:

4 For Gaza shall be forsaken, And Ashkelon desolate; They shall drive out Ashdod at noonday, And Ekron shall be uprooted.

5 Woe to the inhabitants of the seacoast, The nation of the Cherethites! The word of the Lord is against you, O Canaan, land of the Philistines: "I will destroy you; So there shall be no inhabitant. (Zephaniah 2:4-5)

Though there was a partial fulfillment near the time this was written, the time has not yet been when there was no inhabitant in Canaan, hence this prophecy is for the future. Gaza will change and be forsaken! Years ago, because of what Zephaniah 2:4-5 teaches, I concluded that the place of protection Jesus promised the Philadelphians in Revelation 3:10 would NOT be in the direction of Gaza or the land of the Palestinians.

Is Terrorism Prophesied?

The Palestinians, apparently along with some Syrians, are prophesied to be involved in war, apparently a terroristic one:

8 The Lord sent a word against Jacob, And it has fallen on Israel. 9 All the people will know -- Ephraim and the inhabitant of Samaria -- Who say in pride and arrogance of heart: 10 'The bricks have fallen down, But we will rebuild with hewn stones; The sycamores are cut down, But we will replace them with cedars." 11 Therefore the Lord shall set up The adversaries of Rezin against him, And spur his enemies on, 12 The Syrians before and the Philistines behind; And they shall devour Israel with an open mouth. (Isaiah 9:8-12)

Since the above prophecy involves Ephraim and Samaria, this is indicative that the UK (and possibly Canada) and USA (and not just the tiny nation called Israel), respectively, will be attacked. Apparently including terroristic tactics (hitting them before and behind)--though not all Syrians or Palestinians would be part of this.

The Bible shows that terrorism is prophesied:

14 'But if you do not obey Me, and do not observe all these commandments, 15 and if you despise My statutes, or if your soul abhors My judgments, so that you do not perform all My commandments, but break My covenant, 16 I also will do this to you: **I will even appoint terror over you,** wasting disease and fever which shall consume the eyes and cause sorrow of heart. And you shall sow your seed in vain, for your enemies shall eat it. 17 I will set My face against

you, and you shall be defeated by your enemies. Those who hate you shall reign over you, and you shall flee when no one pursues you. (Leviticus 26:14-17)

25 The sword shall destroy outside; **There shall be terror within** (Deuteronomy 32:25)

12 "Cry and wail, son of man; For it will be against My people, Against all the princes of Israel. **Terrors including the sword will be against My people;** Therefore strike your thigh. (Ezekiel 21:12)

12 **Behold, these are the ungodly, Who are always at ease;** They increase in riches...19 **Oh, how they are brought to desolation, as in a moment! They are utterly consumed with terrors.** (Psalms 73:12,19)

25 **Because you disdained all my counsel, And would have none of my rebuke,** 26 I also will laugh at your calamity; **I will mock when your terror comes, 27 When your terror comes like a storm,** And your destruction comes like a whirlwind, When distress and anguish come upon you. (Proverbs 1:25-27)

5 Also **they are afraid of** height, And of **terrors in the way** (Ecclesiastes 12:5).

Jihadist gains in various parts of the world are a prelude to more terrorism and change.

As far as some Palestinian support of terrorism, notice the following:

> A new generation of angry, disillusioned Palestinians is driving the current wave of clashes with Israeli forces . . . some say they want to emulate those killed or wounded in confrontations or attacks on Israelis – like Mohannad Halabi, the 19-year-old law student from the West Bank who stabbed to death two Israelis in Jerusalem's Old City on the weekend before being shot by police.
>
> "We are all impressed by what he has done," said Malik Hussein, the 19-year-old friend and fellow law student at Quds University near Jerusalem. "The day after the attack, university took to the streets and clashed with Israeli soldiers. Mohannad's way is the only way to liberate Palestine." (Daraghmeh M, Laub K. Disillusioned Palestinian youth drive unrest. National Post, October 7, 2015, A1)

Of course, the solution to Palestine and Jerusalem is not war and terrorism, but the return of Jesus Christ and the establishment of the Kingdom of God. Malik Hussein and others should, "Pray for the peace of Jerusalem" (Psalm 122:6).

A confederation against the USA, its Anglo-Saxon allies, and Israel involving Arab and European forces is coming (Psalm 83). And I have long believed that terrorism will have to be part of this.

Goals of Hamas Do Not Include Peace With Israel, But Peace Will--Temporarily--Happen

Gaza is primarily run by a group known as Hamas.

Here is some information about Hamas' official goals:

> THE COVENANT OF THE HAMAS - MAIN POINTS
>
> . . .
>
> Goals of the HAMAS:
>
> --
>
> 'The Islamic Resistance Movement is a distinguished Palestinian movement, whose allegiance is to Allah, and whose way of life is Islam. It strives to raise the banner of Allah over every inch of Palestine.' (Article 6)
>
> On the Destruction of Israel:
>
> --
>
> 'Israel will exist and will continue to exist until Islam will obliterate it, just as it obliterated others before it.' (Preamble)
>
> The Exclusive Moslem Nature of the Area:
>
> --
>
> 'The land of Palestine is an Islamic Waqf [Holy Possession] consecrated for future Moslem generations until Judgment Day. No one can renounce it or any part, or abandon it or any part of it.' (Article 11)
>
> 'Palestine is an Islamic land... Since this is the case, the Liberation of Palestine is an individual duty for every Moslem wherever he may be.' (Article 13)

The Call to Jihad:

'The day the enemies usurp part of Moslem land, Jihad becomes the individual duty of every Moslem. In the face of the Jews' usurpation, it is compulsory that the banner of Jihad be raised.' (Article 15)

'Ranks will close, fighters joining other fighters, and masses everywhere in the Islamic world will come forward in response to the call of duty, loudly proclaiming: 'Hail to Jihad!'. This cry will reach the heavens and will go on being resounded until liberation is achieved, the invaders vanquished and Allah's victory comes about.' (Article 33)

Rejection of a Negotiated Peace Settlement:

'[Peace] initiatives, and so-called peaceful solutions and international conferences are in contradiction to the principles of the Islamic Resistance Movement... Those conferences are no more than a means to appoint the infidels as arbitrators in the lands of Islam...

There is no solution for the Palestinian problem except by Jihad. Initiatives, proposals and international conferences are but a waste of time, an exercise in futility.' (Article 13)

Condemnation of the Israel-Egypt Peace Treaty:

'Egypt was, to a great extent, removed from the circle of struggle [against Zionism] through the treacherous Camp David Agreement. The Zionists are trying to draw other Arab countries into Similar agreements in order to bring them outside the circle of struggle. ...

Leaving the circle of struggle against Zionism is high treason, and cursed be he who perpetrates such an act.' (Article 32) . . . 'The HAMAS regards itself the spearhead and the vanguard of the circle of struggle against World Zionism... Islamic groups all over the Arab world should also do the same, since they are best equipped for their future role in the fight against the warmongering Jews.' (Article 32)

Hamas has more goals, but the above ones give an idea of what it has intended to be about. Hamas is an Islamic organization and has no interest with peace with Israel.

Also, the Palestinian National Authority has stated that it is not interested in US President Donald Trump's peace "deal of the century."

Despite Palestinian claims, a type of temporary "peace deal" will come according to Bible prophecy (Daniel 9:27).

Furthermore, the Palestinian National Authority and Hamas have agreed to temporary cease-fires in the past and, thus, various Palestinians would be expected to do so in the future.

Koran Does Not Teach What Many Muslims Seem to Think?

It may be of interest to note that the area of Palestine is not mentioned in the Koran. Thus, not all Muslims believe that they are to acquire Jerusalem. Notice the following:

> **Sheikh Ahmad Adwan, who introduces himself as a Muslim scholar who lives in Jordan, said on his personal Facebook page that there is no such thing as "Palestine" in the Koran. Allah has assigned the Holy Land to the Children of Israel until the Day of Judgment (Koran, Sura 5 – "The Sura of the Table", Verse 21), and "We made the Children of Israel the inheritors (of the land)" (Koran, Sura 26 – "The Sura of the Poets", Verse 59).**

> "I say to those who distort their Lord's book, the Koran: From where did you bring the name Palestine, you liars, you accursed, when Allah has already named it "The Holy Land" and bequeathed it to the Children of Israel until the Day of Judgment. There is no such thing as 'Palestine' in the Koran. Your demand for the Land of Israel is a falsehood and it constitutes an attack on the Koran, on the Jews and their land. Therefore you won't succeed, and Allah will fail you and humiliate you, because Allah is the one who will protect them (i.e. the Jews)."

The sheikh added: "The Palestinians are the killers of children, the elderly and women. They attack the Jews and then they use those (children, the elderly and women) as human shields and hide behind them, without mercy for their children as if they weren't their own children, in order to tell the public opinion that the Jews intended to kill them. This is exactly what I saw with my own two eyes in the 70's, when they attacked the Jordanian army, which sheltered and protected them. Instead of thanking it (the Jordanian army), they brought their children forward to (face) the Jordanian army, in order to make the world believe that the army kills their children. This is their habit and custom, their viciousness, their having hearts of stones towards their children, and their lying to public opinion, in order to get its support."

It is worth mentioning, that the above mentioned sheikh visited Israel and met Jewish religious scholars. The "Israel in Arabic" site conducted an interview with him, in which he said that the reason for his openness towards the Jewish people "comes from my acknowledgment of their sovereignty on their land and my belief in the Koran, which told us and emphasized this in many places, like His (Allah's) saying "Oh People (i.e the Children of Israel), enter the Holy Land which Allah has assigned unto you" (Koran, Sura 5 – "The Sura of the Table", Verse 21), and His saying "We made the Children of Israel the inheritors (of the land)" (Koran, Sura 26 – "The Sura of the Poets", Verse 59) and many other verses.

He (Adwan) added: "(The Jews) are peaceful people who love peace, who are not hostile and are not aggressors, but if they are attacked, they defend themselves while causing as little damage to the attackers as possible. It is an honor for them that Allah has chosen them over the worlds – meaning over the people and the Jinns until the Day of Judgment. I made the reasons for Allah's choice clear in my books and pamphlets. When Allah chose them, He didn't do so out of politeness, and He wasn't unjust other peoples, it is just that they (the Jews) deserved this." (Cohen E. Jordanian Sheikh: 'There is no "Palestine" in the Koran. Allah gave Israel to the Jews.' Jews News, August 15, 2014)

Of course, just as many people who claim to be Christian believe as doctrines positions contrary to the Bible, Islam has similar issues.

Overall, the Palestinians expect to attain at least part of Jerusalem--and that is consistent with biblical prophecies.

Jebusites?

The Bible tells that King David had the city of the Jebusites, now called Jerusalem taken over:

> 6 And the king and his men went to Jerusalem against the Jebusites, the inhabitants of the land, who spoke to David, saying, "You shall not come in here; but the blind and the lame will repel you," thinking, "David cannot come in here." 7 Nevertheless David took the stronghold of Zion (that is, the City of David).
>
> 8 Now David said on that day, "Whoever climbs up by way of the water shaft and defeats the Jebusites (the lame and the blind, who are hated by David's soul), he shall be chief and captain." Therefore they say, "The blind and the lame shall not come into the house."
>
> 9 Then David dwelt in the stronghold, and called it the City of David. And David built all around from the Millo and inward. 10 So David went on and became great, and the Lord God of hosts was with him. (2 Samuel 5:6-10)

Now after Zedekiah later rebelled, King Nebuchadnezzar's forces took it over and destroyed it in the sixth century B.C.:

> 1 Zedekiah was twenty-one years old when he became king, and he reigned eleven years in Jerusalem. His mother's name was Hamutal the daughter of Jeremiah of Libnah. 2 And he did what was evil in the sight of the Lord, according to all that Jehoiakim had done. 3 For because of the anger of the Lord it came to the point in Jerusalem and Judah that he cast them out from his presence.
>
> And Zedekiah rebelled against the king of Babylon. 4 And in the ninth year of his reign, in the tenth month, on the tenth day of the month,

Nebuchadnezzar king of Babylon came with all his army against Jerusalem, and laid siege to it. And they built siegeworks all around it. 5 So the city was besieged till the eleventh year of King Zedekiah. 6 On the ninth day of the fourth month the famine was so severe in the city that there was no food for the people of the land. 7 Then a breach was made in the city, and all the men of war fled and went out from the city by night by the way of a gate between the two walls, by the king's garden, and the Chaldeans were around the city. And they went in the direction of the Arabah. 8 But the army of the Chaldeans pursued the king and overtook Zedekiah in the plains of Jericho, and all his army was scattered from him. 9 Then they captured the king and brought him up to the king of Babylon at Riblah in the land of Hamath, and he passed sentence on him. 10 The king of Babylon slaughtered the sons of Zedekiah before his eyes, and also slaughtered all the officials of Judah at Riblah. 11 He put out the eyes of Zedekiah, and bound him in chains, and the king of Babylon took him to Babylon, and put him in prison till the day of his death.----

12 In the fifth month, on the tenth day of the month—that was the nineteenth year of King Nebuchadnezzar, king of Babylon—Nebuzaradan the captain of the bodyguard, who served the king of Babylon, entered Jerusalem. 13 And he burned the house of the Lord, and the king's house and all the houses of Jerusalem; every great house he burned down. (Jeremiah 52:1-13, ESV)

What may this have to do with the Palestinians?

Notice also the following:

> The politicians Yasser Arafat and Faisal Husseini among others have claimed that Palestinian Arabs are descended from the Jebusites, in an attempt to argue that Palestinians have a historic claim to Jerusalem that precedes the Jewish one, similar to the more common Palestinian Arab claim that they are descended from the Canaanites. Thus, the 1978 Al-Mawsu'at Al-Filastinniya (Palestinian encyclopedia) asserted, "The Palestinians [are] the descendants of the Jebusites, who are of Arab origin", and described Jerusalem as "an Arab city because its first builders were the Canaanite Jebusites, whose descendants are the Palestinians. (Jebusite. Wikipedia, accessed 12/12/17)

Some dispute the Jebusite connection. Whether or not it is correct, the Jews were certainly not the first peoples in Jerusalem.

Psalm 83, Daniel 11, Ezekiel 30

There are some agreements/confederations that the Palestinians seemingly will be involved in. The one in Psalm 83 specifically includes the Philistines, the modern Palestinians:

> 3 They have taken crafty counsel against Your people, And consulted together against Your sheltered ones. 4 They have said, "Come, and let us cut them off from being a nation, That the name of Israel may be remembered no more." 5 For they have consulted together with one consent; They form a confederacy against You: 6 The tents of Edom and the Ishmaelites; Moab and the Hagrites; 7 Gebal, Ammon, and Amalek; Philistia with the inhabitants of Tyre; 8 Assyria also has joined with them; They have helped the children of Lot. (Psalms 83:3-8)

Notice the following from the old Radio/Worldwide Church of God:

Vast Confederacy...

> Notice especially prophetic Psalm 83. Here we find described a coming coalition of nations of the Middle East whose purpose will be to eradicate the name of Israel! They will say, "Come, and let us cut them off from being a nation; that the name of Israel may be no more in remembrance" (verse 4).
>
> This prophecy could never have been fulfilled {before} this 20th century. Why?
>
> Since ancient times (the 8th century B.C.) there has not been -- until this century -- a nation in the Middle East recognized officially by the name Israel. But there is an Israel today. This is clearly a prophecy for these latter days!
>
> Among the participants in this wide-ranging confederacy revealed in Psalm 83 will be Gebal (ancient Byblos, modern Jubayl) and "the

Philistines [Palestinians centered in the Gaza Strip] with the inhabitants of Tyre" (verse 7).

Here we see that it was anciently — and accurately — prophesied that Palestinian Arabs would in these tumultuous last days become associated in some way with the cities of Lebanon. The prophet Jeremiah (47:4) also speaks of the Philistines and their allies from Tyre and Sidon.

But this prophesied alliance in Psalm 83 will not endure long. The Bible reveals that meanwhile, in our time, a great European military dictator — known in the book of Revelation as the "beast" and in the prophecy of Daniel as the "king of the north" — will arise and ultimately descend upon the Middle East. (Request our free booklet *Who Is the Beast?* for details.)

The beast's intervention will have dire consequences for Israeli and Arab alike. Both Israel ("the glorious land") and Egypt will be occupied by the beast's troops (Dan. 11:40-42). (Stump K. LEBANON'S FUTURE Foretold in the Bible! Plain Truth, September-October 1982)

Notice an amazing prophecy about the Middle East in Psalm 83:1-8. It is a time of war. ... Here is what is yet going to take shape in the Middle East!

"Edom (Turkey), and the Ishmaelites (Saudi Arabia); Moab (part of Jordan), and the Hagarenes (part of Arabia); Gebal (this is the ancient name for Byblos in Lebanon), and Ammon (Jordan) and Amalek (part of the Turks); the Philistines (the displaced Moslems from Palestine) with the inhabitants of Tyre; ASSUR IS JOINED WITH THEM: they have helped the children of Lot." (Hoeh H. GERMANY in Prophecy! - Part 2. Plain Truth, January 1963)

Egypt...will provoke the prophesied United Europe (Dan. 11:40). This European power — called the "king of the north" in Daniel 11 — shall invade and occupy the "glorious land" of Palestine (verse 41). "And the land of Egypt shall not escape"(Boraker R. SYRIA RAIDS ISRAEL — Where Is It Leading? Plain Truth. November 1966)

Notice also from Catholic and Protestant translations of Ezekiel:

5 Cush, Put and Lud, all Arabia, Cub and the children of the country of the covenant will fall by the sword with them. (Ezekiel 30:5, NJB)

5 "Ethiopia, Libya, Lydia, all the mingled people, Chub, and the men of the lands who are allied, shall fall with them by the sword." (Ezekiel 30:5)

What is the "country of the covenant"? Why, that must be the land promised to Abraham, but specifically would also include the land dominated by the nation of Israel. The above then would seem to have to include the Palestinians, including those of Gaza.

Also, since the Gazites/Palestinians seem to be related to the other Arabic peoples, prophecies related to the Arabic peoples will also apply, such as Ezekiel 30:2-8.

There have been rockets, retaliations, and other fighting between Israel and the Palestinian Gazites. Although there have been temporary cease-fires, it has been stated that, "Neither side appeared ready to accept the other's conditions for a permanent cease-fire" (http://www.voanews.com/content/israel-hamas-resume-fighting-as-cairo-talks-break-down/2419518.html). A multi-year temporary peace deal will come about per Daniel 9:27, and that seems consistent with what those in Gaza and Israel may (after more pressure) be willing to accept.

Biblical prophecy teaches that the Palestinians of Gaza and the West Bank will support confederations which will not end well in this age. They will, for a time, believe that they will be protected by a temporary "peace deal' (Daniel 9:27) and other international arrangements (Daniel 11:27; Psalm 83:3-8) that will not end well (Daniel 11:31,40-43; Ezekiel 30:2-9) according to biblical, and even Islamic prophecy.

That being said, Jesus will come and straighten this world out (see also our free booklet *The Gospel of the Kingdom of God*).

The Bible also tells of an age to come and that all that ever lived, Palestin, Gazite, or not, will be offered salvation (see also our free book *Universal OFFER of Salvation, Apokatastasis: Can God save the lost in an age to come? Hundreds of scriptures reveal God's plan of salvation*).

Until then, we can expect problems to come to Gaza and other parts of Palestine.

The FIFTH Commandment

By Bob Thiel

When Adam and Eve sinned, they also dishonored their only parent.

In the New Testament Adam is called the "son of God" (Luke 3:38). This is because God created him. Adam was the son of God by a direct creation. Adam was not God's son by regular human begettal or birth. Eve, was fashioned by God out of Adam's rib (Genesis 2:21-23), and hence was not born the usual way.

Adam not only dishonored God, but he also broke the tenth commandment. There was also lust when the woman felt the forbidden fruit was good for food and desired to make one wise; vanity, egotism and pride entered into her heart (Genesis 3:6) which would violate the ninth commandment. She put the word of the serpent over the word of God and hence violated the first commandment. She made an idol out of worldly wisdom (cf. 1 Corinthians 3:19) and thus violated the second commandment.

Lust is what usually causes a person to have an inordinate desire to have something that is not to be theirs. Lust can cause some to steal, and Adam and Eve broke the eighth commandment by stealing what was not theirs to take.

At least six of the Ten Commandments were broken when Eve partook of the forbidden fruit.

And in other ways every one of the Ten Commandments was actually broken in that first human sin. Improperly disobeying parents can lead to many problems.

The fifth commandment, from the Book of Exodus, states:

> 12 "Honor your father and your mother, that your days may be long upon the land which the Lord your God is giving you. (Exodus 20:12)

The version in Deuteronomy is a bit longer:

> 16 'Honor your father and your mother, as the Lord your God has commanded you, that your days may be long, and that it may be well with you in the land which the Lord your God is giving you. (Deuteronomy 5:16)

Deuteronomy means "second law" and all the Ten Commandments are repeated in the 5th chapter of Deuteronomy.

If children would honor their parents and parents were honorable, it would go well in the physical land.

A disobedient child is a frustrated child as that child's mind is often plagued with feelings of guilt and rebellion. Children who love, honor, and obey their parents are blessed.

In modern times, it is also realized that those who come from more stable families are less likely to be involved in crime.

Children are to Be Taught

Children do not naturally know how to do right and they need to be taught.

One of the biggest "secrets" of being a successful parent is to spend time with your child(ren).

Those that follow what the Bible teaches will teach their children. Notice what the Bible shows God said right after Moses reiterated the Ten Commandments in Deuteronomy:

> 6 "And these words which I command you today shall be in your heart. 7 You shall teach them diligently to your children, and shall talk of them when you sit in your house, when you walk by the way, when you lie down, and when you rise up. 8 You shall bind them as a sign on your hand,

and they shall be as frontlets between your eyes. 9 You shall write them on the doorposts of your house and on your gates. (Deuteronomy 6:6-9)

6 Train up a child in the way he should go, And when he is old he will not depart from it. (Proverbs 22:6).

Children who learn God's words and commands will learn about what is right.

When children have proper boundaries and are taught right from wrong as the Bible teaches, they can avoid many pitfalls in the world. They also will tend to be happier (cf. Psalm 144:15; Proverbs 28:14).

The Bible also teaches:

3 Behold, children are a heritage from the Lord, The fruit of the womb is a reward. 4 Like arrows in the hand of a warrior, So are the children of one's youth. 5 Happy is the man who has his quiver full of them; they shall not be ashamed, But shall speak with their enemies in the gate. (Psalm 127:3-5)

Parents should properly correct their children. The Bible teaches:

13 Don't fail to discipline your children. They won't die if you spank them. (Proverbs 23:13, New Living Translation, NLT)

10 Harsh discipline is for him who forsakes the way, And he who hates correction will die. (Proverbs 15:10)

17 Correct your son, and he will give you rest; Yes, he will give delight to your soul. (Proverbs 29:17)

Most children should not need much in the way of "harsh" discipline. And in modern society, be cautious about the wisdom of spanking (legally it is not allowed in various countries). But children should have rules and boundaries and be subject to discipline if they violate those rules and boundaries.

There are many ways to provide discipline to your children. Talking with them, removing or restricting privileges, as well as my favorite: giving children additional work to do. Having children pull weeds was one of this author's favorite forms of disciplinary punishment.

Also, as they get older, properly raised children normally will respond to simply expressing your disappointment in them as sufficient discipline.

Consider also that the Bible teaches, "And the hope of the hypocrite shall perish" (Job 8:13)--if you hope that your children will turn out well, then try not to live as a hypocrite. Not being a hypocrite goes a long way in helping parents to be honorable.

Does the fifth commandment mean that children must obey their parents if they are told to violate God's law?

No. "We ought to obey God rather than men" (Acts 5:29). But honorable parents will not tell their children to disobey God's laws.

Are children to obey dishonorable parents in other ways? That depends, but overall children are to honor their parents, whether they are honorable or not. Parents are to act honorably whether their children honor them or not.

Teaching Children Helps Them

The Book of Proverbs repeatedly mentions that it is good for children to listen to their parents:

8 My son, hear the instruction of your father, And do not forsake the law of your mother; 9 For they will be a graceful ornament on your head, And chains about your neck. (Proverbs 1:8-9)

1 Hear, my children, the instruction of a father, And give attention to know understanding; 2 For I give you good doctrine: Do not forsake my law. 3 When I was my father's son, Tender and the only one in the sight of my mother, 4 He also taught me, and said to me: "Let your heart retain my words; Keep my commands, and live. (Proverbs 4:1-4)

20 My son, keep your father's command, And do not forsake the law of your mother. 21 Bind them continually upon your heart; Tie them around your neck. 22 When you roam, they will lead you; When you sleep, they will keep you; And when you awake, they will speak with you. 23 For the

commandment is a lamp, And the law a light; Reproofs of instruction are the way of life, 24 To keep you from the evil woman, From the flattering tongue of a seductress. (Proverbs 6:20-24)

The Bible teaches that children should listen to good advice from their parents. Notice also:

> 1 Children, obey your parents in the Lord, for this is right. (Ephesians 6:1)

Children are not to obey if parents tell them to violate God's law.

Adult Children

Adult children should be polite to their parents, when possible, whether or not they are particularly honorable.

Proverbs teaches:

> 26 He who mistreats his father and chases away his mother Is a son who causes shame and brings reproach. (Proverbs 19:26)

> 22 Listen to your father who begot you, And do not despise your mother when she is old. (Proverbs 23:22)

It is normally advisable for adults to attempt to maintain at least some contact with parents—though this does not mean compromising on holy days or the world's holidays.

In biblical times, adult children were also expected to financially support their parents when they were elderly.

The Pharisees tried to reason around this, but notice what Jesus taught:

> 9 He said to them, "All too well you reject the commandment of God, that you may keep your tradition. 10 For Moses said, 'Honor your father and your mother'; and, 'He who curses father or mother, let him be put to death.' 11 But you say, 'If a man says to his father or mother, "Whatever profit you might have received from me is Corban" — ' (that is, a gift to God), 12 then you no longer let him do anything for his father or his mother, 13 making the word of God of no effect through your tradition which you have handed down. And many such things you do." (Mark 7:9-13)

What about today?

Do adult children have any financial obligations to support their parents?

Yes (cf. 1 Timothy 5:8).

However, in the case of many Western societies, it often is unnecessary. Yet, if it is necessary, adult children still have that obligation.

But what about enabling destructive behavior?

If a parent is a drug-addict, an alcoholic, pornography addict, purposely deceitful, or otherwise is participating in harmful behaviors, should adult children enable this?

No (cf. Galatians 6:1-2; Proverbs 23:20-21; 30:15; 2 Thessalonians 3:10-12; Matthew 18:6). Consider also:

> 11 And have no fellowship with the unfruitful works of darkness, but rather expose them. (Ephesians 5:11)

Hence, while food, clothing, and lodging may need to be provided by adult children, "cash-money" to a parent who would tend to improperly spend on bad behaviors is not something anyone should give.

Furthermore, while you are to honor your parents, understand that Jesus taught against putting family considerations/traditions above following Him (Matthew 10:37; 15:3-9).

Fifth Commandment Before Sinai, from Jesus, and After Jesus' Death

The Bible shows the fifth commandment was in place before Mt. Sinai:

> "Adam, the son of God" (Luke 3:38), "Because you have heeded the voice of your wife, and eaten from the tree of which I commanded you, saying, 'You shall not eat it of it': Cursed is the ground

for your sake" (Genesis 3:17). "Now therefore, my son, obey my voice" (Genesis 27:43). "Jacob had obeyed his father and his mother" (Genesis 28:7). Notice that later a blessing of land is promised for those who obey this commandment (Exodus 20:12; Deuteronomy 5:16).

Jesus taught and expanded the fifth commandment:

"For God commanded saying, 'Honor your father and your mother' and 'He who curses father or mother, let him be put to death'" (Matthew 15:4). "Honor your father and your mother" (Matthew 19:19). "Honor your father and your mother" (Mark 7:10). "Honor your father and your mother" (Mark 10:19). "You know the commandments: ... Honor your father and your mother" (Luke 18:20).

After Jesus was resurrected, the New Testament taught the fifth commandment:

"being filled with all unrighteousness ... disobedient to parents" (Romans 1:29,30). "Children obey your parents in the Lord, for this is right. 'Honor your father and mother', which is the first commandment with promise: that it may be well with you and you may live long on the earth" (Ephesians 6:1-3). "the wrath of God is coming upon the sons of disobedience" (Colossians 3:6). "Children obey your parents in all things, for this is well pleasing to the Lord" (Colossians 3:20). "But know this, that in the last days perilous times will come: For men will be...disobedient to parents" (2 Timothy 3:1,2). "Therefore gird up the loins of your mind, be sober, ... as obedient children" (1 Peter 1:13-14). "They have a heart trained in covetous practices and are accursed children" (2 Peter 2:14). "Behold what manner of love the Father has bestowed upon us, that we should be called children of God" (1 John 3:1).

The world would be a much nicer place if children would honor their parents and the parents made themselves more honorable.

More on the Ten Commandments can be found in our free online book, available at www.ccog.org, titled: 'The Ten Commandments: The Decalogue, Christianity, and the Beast.'

STUDY THE BIBLE COURSE

Lesson 16b: You Must Be Born Again

Published 2019 by the *Continuing* Church of God

Preface: This course is highly based upon the personal correspondence course developed in 1954 that began under the direction of the late C. Paul Meredith in the old Radio Church of God. Various portions have been updated for the 21st century (though much of the original writing has been retained). It also has more scriptural references, as well as information and questions not in the original course. Unless otherwise noted, scriptural references are to the NKJV, copyright Thomas Nelson Publishing, used by permission. The KJV, sometimes referred to as the Authorized Version is also often used. Additionally, Catholic-approved translations such as the New Jerusalem Bible (NJB) are sometimes used as are other translations.

How to Receive the Holy Spirit

Since Jesus makes the physical birth a TYPE of the spiritual, let's compare the similarities of these two DIFFERENT births which each one must experience in order to be saved.

Physically speaking, you became a child of your parents at the very instant of conception when a new physical life was begun. At that time you were conceived, or begotten, but not yet born. But you were your parents' child just as much as Jacob and

Esau were their parents' children BEFORE birth: "for the CHILDREN NOT YET BEING BORN …" (Romans 9:11).

IN THE SAME MANNER, if you are a real Christian, you are now a BEGOTTEN child or son of God. Upon conversion, God the Father placed within you His Spirit, THE GERM or SPERM, so to speak, of eternal life. HE BEGOT YOU WITH THE HOLY SPIRIT JUST AS THE SPERM FROM A HUMAN FATHER IMPREGNATES THE EGG OF THE MOTHER. Your mind is like an egg. You needed to be impregnated with the germ of eternal life to BEGIN the process of spiritual growth. But you are NOT YET BORN of God – NOT YET COMPOSED OF SPIRIT – NOT YET IMMORTAL.

As the unborn son or daughter is nourished and protected by its MOTHER for a period of time, at the end of which period it is born, if it has grown properly, so it is the FUNCTION OF THE TRUE CHURCH – the "MOTHER of us all" – to feed true Christians with the pure Word of God. Thus you must be NOURISHED as God's child on spiritual food – the words of Scripture – you must LIVE by every word of God – you must GROW spiritually (2 Peter 3:18) – until you are mature enough in righteous character to be BORN of God.

But how is it all possible? How do we receive the Holy Spirit which makes us the children of God and makes possible the beginning of eternal life within us? Understand.

1. IS REPENTANCE one of the requirements for receiving the Holy Spirit? Acts 2:38. What is repentance? Notice 2 Corinthians 7:9-10 for the answer.

COMMENT: In Acts 2:38, baptism is mentioned as part of the prior condition to receiving the gift of the Holy Spirit from God. The entire subject of water baptism will be presented in two future lessons.

2. Is the Holy Spirit a GIFT from God – or is it something we were born with by nature? Compare Luke 11:13 with Acts 10:45.

3. Then the Holy Spirit is NOT something we already have – NOT something we were born with, is it? Acts 11:16-17.

4. Are we to ASK GOD TO GRANT us the Holy Spirit? Luke 11:13 again.

5. How can we know that God HEARS US when we ask Him for His Holy Spirit? 1 John 3:22. Doesn't keeping the commandments and doing the things that please God satisfy His requirements? Same verse.

COMMENT: We must have REPENTED of having lived by our OWN ways – our own standards or laws – and now have made a complete change of direction. Now we must be so desirous of pleasing God that we are keeping HIS COMMANDMENTS as much as we are HUMANLY able to do with our weak, carnal, fleshly minds. THEN, when we ask God to be begotten of Him (as our spiritual Heavenly Father) by the Spirit of POWER which will enable us to truly keep His commands in their highest SPIRITUAL sense, He will HEAR US and impregnate us – the egg – with His very Spirit which will help to gradually change our carnal natures until we are finally BORN of God at the resurrection!

6. Does Acts 5:32 also verify the fact that OBEDIENCE is one of the conditions to receiving the Holy Spirit – one of the conditions to receiving the gift of eternal life?

COMMENT: The Holy Spirit is a freely offered GIFT from God. It is NOT ANYTHING WE CAN EARN. There is nothing you can do which will force God to give you the Holy Spirit. Rather, God offers to give you freely of His Spirit if you will believe in the sacrifice of His Son, Jesus Christ, for your sins and become willing to DO what He commands you. These are prior conditions, but they DO NOT EARN YOU eternal life.

A Counterfeit Spirit Preached

Most people are totally unaware of Paul's WARNING that there would be many false churches preaching DIFFERENT doctrines about the Holy Spirit – DECEIVING THE MANY into accepting a DIFFERENT spirit from the one, true Holy Spirit revealed in Scripture, which ALONE can beget eternal life within us!

Notice: "But I fear" – Paul was sorrowed, he knew what was coming in our day – "lest somehow, as the SERPENT beguiled Eve in his craftiness, YOUR thoughts should be corrupted from the SIMPLICITY and the purity that is toward the Christ" (2 Corinthians 11:3, "Panin" Translation.). Christ's doctrine is SIMPLE, when we understand it — it is not a theological mystery!

Continuing with verse 4 (Panin Translation): "For if he who cometh" – any false minister coming in the name of Christ, "preacheth ANOTHER Jesus" – the world is filled with the preaching of a DIFFERENT Jesus who was born, who died and rose at a different time than the true Messiah; a different Jesus who rejected the Father's immutable laws – "whom we did not preach" – says Paul – "or ye receive a different spirit, which ye did not receive" – from the preaching of the apostles – "ye bear well with him –" or accept or are DECEIVED by him.

That is what has happened today. Paul warned about receiving a "different spirit" and "a different gospel."

This prophetic warning from Paul has, sadly, already been fulfilled! The world has accepted a DIFFERENT spirit – THE SPIRIT OF ERROR, not the spirit of truth.

The Apostle Paul further warned that Satan's ministers would deceptively appear to transform themselves into "ministers of righteousness" (2 Corinthians 11:14-15).

Ecclesiastical history, in and out of the Bible, shows that those who did so had success in deceiving many.

Most churches have some truth, but it is the true "Church of God" that is the "pillar and ground of the truth" (1 Timothy 3:15). Satan, the god of this age (2 Corinthians 4:4), appears, not as the devil, but as an angel of light to many (2 Corinthians 11:13-14). Jesus said many would come in His name, proclaiming that He was the Christ — and yet, without realizing it, deceiving the whole world (Matthew 24:4-5).

In a misguided attempt towards peace, many religious and political leaders in the 21st century are promoting the "spirit of error" in many aspects of ecumenical and interfaith movements. The ecumenical movement tries to consider that all professed Christian faiths are equal before God, yet the Bible warns about false ministers (2 Corinthians 11:14-15) and a false "Mystery Babylonian" faith that involves the world's political leaders (Revelation 17:1- 9). Jesus did not come to bring international unity in this age, but division (Luke 12:51). Christians are to flee from the prophesied Babylon (Zechariah 2;6-7; Revelation 18:4) and be unspotted by the world (James 1:27).

1. How can we know that we have received the true spirit of God and not some counterfeit spirit from the devil? Notice the principle recorded in Matthew 7:20. We can KNOW which ministers are preaching about the Spirit of God BY THE FRUITS of the Spirit in their lives, can't we?

2. What is the FRUIT of the TRUE Spirit of God? Galatians 5:22-23.

3. What is the first one of the fruits listed – the most important fruit? Is it love? Same verse and 1 Corinthians 13:13.

4. Is the love of God one of the manifestations of the Holy Spirit? Romans 5:5. Isn't it clear that a person does not have the love of God if he does not have the Holy Spirit dwelling in him?

5. What is the love of God? Romans 13:10. Is not this the same teaching we discovered in 1 John 3:22-23? This has been God's message from the beginning, hasn't it? 1 John 3:11-12.

COMMENT: Before one can receive the Holy Spirit, one must have the attitude of obedience. One must become willing to do God's will – obey God's commandments. BUT IT IS NOT UNTIL SOMEONE HAS RECEIVED THE HOLY SPIRIT THAT HE/SHE OBTAINS THE POWER TO PERFORM GOD'S LAW. The Holy Spirit is the POWER of God manifest in our lives (Romans 15:13).

The other fruits of the Spirit, mentioned by Paul in Galatians 5:22, amplify the attitude of love. Obedience to God is not harsh and cruel and unyielding – it is a joy, it is peaceable and gentle, it expresses itself in SELF-CONTROL. Self-control is the key to real spiritual power. Most people cannot be filled with spiritual power because they have not been willing to exercise self-control. Uncontrolled power is worse than no power at all.

You have probably been taught that you cannot receive the Holy Spirit until you work up your emotions or until you reject God's law. That deceptive teaching results from hearing a PERVERTED gospel – a DIFFERENT gospel than Jesus preached.

Begotten Now – Not Yet Born of God

The Holy Spirit, which a person may receive if he asks God for it, in conformity to His will, MAY BE COMPARED TO the GERM or SPERM of physical life. IT TRANSMITS GOD'S MENTAL POWERS AND SPIRITUAL ATTRIBUTES TO US. It is His LOVE. It is His divine NATURE. It is His immortal life.

First, notice that the Holy Spirit – the germ by which we are begotten – comes from the Father. God has masculine characteristics. That is why we call Him "Father." We are called the BEGOTTEN children of God (1 John 3:1). God, then, has the power to BEGET US as His children. HE BEGETS US "BY HIS SPIRIT." The Spirit by which we are begotten is termed in the Bible a GERM or "seed." Peter tells us we are "begotten again, not of corruptible seed, but of incorruptible, through God's Word, which liveth and abideth" (1 Peter 1:23 "Ivan Panin" trans.). Jesus completes this by saying we must FINALLY BE BORN AGAIN – at the resurrection – when we shall be spirit. Now we are ONLY FLESH with the spiritual germ of eternal life EMPOWERING US.

Now consider the full scriptural PROOF that we are only the BEGOTTEN children of God, not yet born of Him.

1. Are we already called the "sons of God"? Compare Romans 8:14 with 1 John 3:1.

2. Does being a son of God mean that we are already BORN of God, OR are we ONLY BEGOTTEN of Him now? 1 Peter 1:23.

COMMENT: ONE Greek word means BOTH "BEGOTTEN" AND "BORN." The translators unfortunately, at times, selected the wrong one of these two words when translating a Bible sentence, so that the English word "born" may appear where "begotten" is intended, and vice versa.

anagennaō. The KJV translates Strong's G313 in the following manner: begat again (1x), be born again (1x).

But What About 1 Peter 1:23?

Some have wondered about the following passage and suggest this is proof that Christians are already born again:

> 23 having been born again, not of corruptible seed but incorruptible, through the word of God which lives and abides forever, (1 Peter 1:23, NKJV)

But the above does not properly convey the intent of the writing. The translation of that is misleading.

It should state that we have been BEGOTTEN again, as we have not yet been born into the kingdom.

Notice three translations that get this right:

> 23 having been begotten again, not of corruptible seed, but of incorruptible, through the word of God, which liveth and abideth. (1 Peter 1:23 American Standard Version)

> 23 For you have been begotten again, not from corruptible seed, but from incorruptible seed, by the living Word of God, which remains forever. (1 Peter 1:23, A Faithful Version)

> 23 being begotten again, not out of seed corruptible, but incorruptible, through a word of God -- living and remaining -- to the age; (1 Peter 1:23 Young's Literal Translation).

In this age Christians are begotten by the Holy Spirit to be born again in the resurrection.

3. If we are the children of God, are we inheritors of the Kingdom of God, or only HEIRS to it? Romans 8:17.

COMMENT: Notice that although we are now the sons of God, we are only HEIRS. Why? BECAUSE WE ARE ONLY BEGOTTEN children. We shall be INHERITORS WHEN BORN of God at the resurrection, when we shall be composed of spirit.

WHATEVER IS BORN OF SPIRIT IS SPIRIT, said Jesus. We are not yet born of spirit. We are STILL FLESH AND BLOOD! We are therefore only HEIRS to the kingdom of God (1 Corinthians 15:50).

4. When do we become incorruptible spirit and no longer flesh? 1 Corinthians 15:42. Has the resurrection of the dead occurred yet? Then we are NOT YET born into the Kingdom of God as inheritors, are we?

We are only the begotten children of God!

5. Are we ALREADY like Christ in appearance and in composition? 1 John 3:1-2, KJV. When WILL we be like Him? – when He appears to raise the dead? Verse 2, KJV. We are only BEGOTTEN sons now.

COMMENT: We are begotten of God, impregnated by the Holy Spirit from the Father, which is the beginning of eternal life. But we are not yet born of Him, for it has not yet appeared what we shall be like. We do NOT look like Christ now. Note the point that John emphasizes. We shall be like Him, COMPOSED of Spirit – "that which is born of the Spirit is spirit" – "when He shall appear" – at the resurrection when Christ returns to raise the dead.

Then we shall see Jesus as He really is. Christ told Nicodemus that in order to see the Kingdom or Family of God, in which He – Christ – now is, we must be born again. How consistent the teaching of the Bible is!

When we are born again, composed of spirit, we shall be able to SEE spirit – we shall BEHOLD Jesus Christ as He ACTUALLY appears. But the people of the world, who will still be composed of FLESH and can't see spirit, will see Christ only as He PHYSICALLY manifests Himself in glorious form at His return.

We Receive "Spirit of Sonship"

1. Is God called the "FATHER of spirits"? Hebrews 12:9. Then does this not clearly prove that we can be finally literally be BORN of God? – be born as His SPIRIT-COMPOSED CHILDREN?

2. Is Christ called the "FIRSTBORN among MANY BRETHREN"? Romans 8:29. Since He is the first Son BORN into the God-Kingdom, then there must BE OTHER SONS also TO BE BORN into it.

Does not this same verse clearly explain that we are to be like Christ – "conformed to the image of His Son" – that we are to be His brethren?

COMMENT: PRIOR to THE DEATH AND RESURRECTION OF JESUS CHRIST, He was the ONLY begotten Son of the Father, BUT SINCE THAT TIME WE ALSO MAY BE BEGOTTEN OF THE FATHER.

3. IS JESUS CHRIST declared to be the firstborn from the dead? Colossians 1:18. Since He is the FIRSTborn from the dead, then are the OTHERS who are to be raised from the dead also to be born into the Kingdom of God as Jesus has been? How else could He be the firstborn?

4. Are Christians called the CHILDREN of God? Galatians 3:26, KJV.

5. Now compare Galatians 3:26 with Romans 8:14-17 and Ephesians 1:5. Do these verses reveal the SAME truth – that we are to be born again in order to inherit eternal life?

COMMENT: In some versions of the Bible the expression "adoption of sons" or "adoption of children" is used. This is not a proper translation. The original inspired Greek expression "huiothesia" means sonship. WE RECEIVE THE "SPIRIT OF SONSHIP," not the "spirit of ADOPTION." The Holy Spirit makes us LITERAL SONS OF GOD. WE ARE GOING TO BE LIKE OUR HEAVENLY FATHER. What is the NAME which all truly begotten children of God bear as a result of receiving the Holy Spirit from the Father? Ephesians 3:14-15.

COMMENT: The name which all converts bear as a result of being begotten by the Holy Spirit is "God."

We are called the "sons of God" or "God's sons" – just as human beings bear the names Johnson, Robertson, and Jackson, meaning originally the sons of John, Robert and of Jack. GOD is the FAMILY NAME of the divine Kingdom. It is the Father "from whom the whole family in heaven and earth is named" (Ephesians 3:15).

Notice what the very first words of the Bible tell us about God?

> 1 In the beginning God created the heavens and the earth. (Genesis 1:1, NKJV throughout unless as otherwise noted)

The original Hebrew word translated God in verse 1 is Elohim. Elohim is a uniplural or collective noun, like the words church, family and kingdom.

In other words, the term Elohim stands for a group composed of two or more individuals. Elohim in Genesis 1:1 means the God Family.

Both the Father and Son are God:

> 2 that their hearts may be encouraged, being knit together in love, and attaining to all riches of the full assurance of understanding, to the knowledge of the mystery of God, both of the Father and of Christ, 3 in whom are hidden all the treasures of wisdom and knowledge. (Colossians 2:2-3)

Jesus is called God in John 1:1 and in other verses. He is not angelic spirit, but divine or GOD Spirit.

God is a GROWING Family or Kingdom into which we may enter. God is a Family, a Kingdom, NOT A TRINITY. The Father in Heaven wants you to become a member of His divine Family. You can be His son if you surrender your whole life to Him – believe all that is in the Bible – believe Christ is your Saviour and obey Him – and be filled with the power of the Spirit of God.

SPIRITUAL THINGS seem unreal to most people. And no wonder! Spiritual qualities are invisible, not discerned by the senses until revealed in writing in the Bible!

When we speak of the Holy Spirit, many cannot grasp its nature. Yet the Bible makes clear the nature of spirit.

Notice, "God is Spirit" (John 4:24). The God-Family is composed of spirit. The Father and the Son, who are already composed of spirit, have definite SHAPE. From one end of the Bible to the other we are told about the SHAPE and the parts of each member in the God-Family. The Father and the Son each have a head, hair, eyes, nose, mouth, arms, fingers, a torso, legs, feet, (Daniel 7:9; Ezekiel 1:26-28; Revelation 1:13-16) plus inward parts (e.g. Genesis 6:5-6). So has man. Man is in the IMAGE of God (Genesis 1:26). But man is born only of flesh. Man is matter, but God is spirit. (Review the lesson titled "Are Humans Immortal?", Lesson 14. You will now learn things you didn't see in that lesson before!)

Even though the Father and the Son are spirit and are in definite locations with respect to each other, the Spirit proceeds from them into the entire universe much like air fills everything on earth! Note David's words that God's Spirit permeates EVERYTHING. (Psalm 139:7-11.)

The divine Spirit that fills the entire universe is the channel by which the Father and the Son create. HUMANS HAVE NO SUCH DIVINE ATTRIBUTE OR POWER BORN INTO THEM. But humans may FORM TOOLS and electronic brains to make things.

Humans were put here on earth to LEARN to develop tools for limited creative work – to train for the eternal goal – becoming part of the GOD-FAMILY, which means SHARING control of the creative Spirit of God in order to help eternity be better.

That is what it means to become born again – to be fully imbued with God's power when composed of Spirit.

To Become PERFECT When Born of God

Only when one is BORN of God by a resurrection does a person become PERFECT (1 John 3:9). Christ is the only human being thus far BORN of God. He is PERFECT.

Of course! If we are God's children, we are to "GROW UP" to become like Him.

The Eternal God has created innumerable galaxies of stars and planets. The full extent of His entire finished creation is completely beyond the grasp of the human mind – completely beyond the telescope or the microscope.

But wonder of wonders! – GOD IS STILL CREATING BEFORE OUR VERY EYES HIS HIGHEST AND NOBLEST WORK – He is fashioning begotten sons to be BORN INTO HIS OWN FAMILY! YOU and I have the opportunity of becoming a son in the Family or Kingdom of God!

By a process completely hidden to the world, and revealed only to His own children by the Bible, God is now begetting, through the operation of the Holy Spirit, sons AFTER HIS OWN KIND – after His own character and likeness. The begettal, nourishment and actual birth of sons into the God Kingdom by a resurrection to divine and glorified immortality is THE SUPREME PINNACLE OF CREATION – GOD THE CREATOR'S SUPREME ACHIEVEMENT!

Yet most churches do not realize this wonderful truth. They talk about being born of God, but they DON'T KNOW WHAT IT MEANS!

1. Are Christians to have the very MIND of God? Philippians 2:5. Did Jesus Christ have that mind in Him when He walked on earth? Same verse.

2. Are humans naturally born with the mind of God? Romans 8:6-7. Is the human mind naturally subject to the laws of God?

3. What is the natural mind of man like? Mark 7:21-22, Matthew 15:19 and Jeremiah 17:9.

4. Are we commanded to surrender our natural, carnal minds to God? Galatians 5:16-17. Are we to yield our minds to the influence of the Spirit of God? Same verses.

5. Are the laws of God to be ingrained in our minds if we are Christians? Hebrews 8:8-11. Isn't it clear that one of the final characteristics of Christians who are now begotten and finally will be born of God is that they will have become like God in character – perfect – unable to sin? Note especially verse 10 and 1 John 3:9.

One Other Point

It has been the favorite teaching of some that Christians can't sin anymore in this life because they are "born again". This doctrine originated from misapplying 1 John 3:9: "Whoever has been born of God does not sin, for His seed remains in him; and he cannot sin, because he has been born of God." Notice what this means.

1. Can Christians commit sin? 1 John 1:8. Who is doing the speaking in this verse the apostle John? And is he using the present tense of the verb? Then the apostle plainly means that Christians now can, and sometimes do commit SIN, doesn't he? Notice that he includes HIMSELF – "WE".

2. Was the apostle Paul beset with recurring sin long AFTER he repented and received the Holy Spirit? Romans 7:14-25.

3. Does Jesus admonish us to overcome sin continually? Revelation 2:26.

4. Is there a just man on earth who does not at some time commit sin? Ecclesiastes 7:20. Therefore Christians are NOT now born of God in this mortal flesh, are they?

5. Now notice 1 John 5:18, KJV. What does this scripture reveal?

COMMENT: Notice the difference between the two conditions referred to in this verse. The one CAN'T sin because God's "seed remaineth in him". One is BORN of God and has God's nature, NOT the human nature that once caused one to sin if that person didn't have the strength to resist. The other, who is BEGOTTEN, must keep from being spotted – that one must continue to RESIST the deceptions and the pollutions of the world. Such a one CAN commit sin – YET WILL NOT WILLFULLY SIN – BUT WHEN CAUGHT OFF GUARD OR IN A MOMENT OF WEAKNESS – CAN SIN. Life is to the begotten child still a CONSTANT STRUGGLE against the wiles of the devil operating in the world and through his own human nature. Although the Christian has now received THE DIVINE NATURE (2 Peter 1:4), the Christian still has HUMAN NATURE, and the one wars against the other. Christians must keep their human nature "crucified" like Him (Romans 6:6) – and WILL to be LED BY the Spirit or nature of God. (Ephesians 3:20; Romans 8:14.)

Much of the confusion about being born again has resulted from misinterpreting the original Greek.

In the English language we have two different verbs – TO BEGET and TO BE BORN – which are used to translate the ONE Greek word GENNAO. This Greek word means "to conceive", or "to beget", and also "to bear," or "to be born." In order to know which meaning is intended, we must let the Bible interpret the Bible. Since the Bible plainly reveals that Christians can sin now – in this flesh-and-blood mortal existence – we therefore KNOW that it is only when one is actually BORN OF GOD IN THE FUTURE, at the resurrection, that he CANNOT sin anymore.

SUMMARY

In summary, the Holy Spirit of God is this: It is the very spirit – the very LIFE, the very ESSENCE of God the Creator! God, according to John 4:24, is Spirit. But man is mortal. Humans are flesh. God is composed of Spirit. Spirit is not like matter. Humans are composed of matter. Matter occupies a definite amount of physical space, and has weight. But God's Spirit emanates from Him, like the air. It is force. It is POWER, it is LIFE, it is CHARACTER!

When God's Spirit, emanating from the very person of God, enters into a human, it IMPREGNATES that human's mind with the very LIFE OF GOD. It plants within that man or woman the divine nature of God, to develop the very character of God, until we, through His Spirit, BECOME LIKE GOD – until we THINK as God thinks – until we see things with the same attitude as God sees them, and we act as God acts – yes, until we BECOME GOD even as Christ is now VERY GOD – BORN MEMBERS OF THE GOD FAMILY which is THE KINGDOM OF GOD!

What WONDERFUL NEWS! What meaning there is to being "born again"!

Editor: Since that article came out, more and more studies have demonstrated that proper exercise improves longevity and reduces the risk for numerous diseases. Furthermore, exercise can help one feel younger and be able to be more productive in one's later years.

FREE *Continuing Church of God* Books and Booklets
at www.ccog.org/books

Christians: AMBASSADORS

Continuing History of the Church of God

Dating: A Key to Success in Marriage

Faith for Those God has Called and Chosen

The Gospel of the Kingdom of God

Is God Calling You?

Is God's Existence Logical?

Prayer: What Does the Bible Teach?

Artist portrayal of King Solomon by Isaak L'vovich Asknaziy

Happiness Is ...

By Charles F. Vinson

This article was originally published in the January 1973 edition of the Plain Truth magazine.

How MANY times have you thought, I'd be happy , if only . ... ? The daydream usually continues with " If only I had more money", or, "if only I had married someone else", or, "if only I could change jobs", or, "if only I had better health".

Always "if only".

Is happiness the impossible dream? Why does it always seem to be somewhere around the corner, off in the vague future , but never really right now?

Certainly there are reasons enough for the world's all-too-common victims of war, disease, hunger and poverty to be less than satisfied with living. But what makes most Americans, Britons, Japanese, Germans - peoples who, in the main, enjoy a higher degree of human comfort than most of the other peoples of the world - so often dissatisfied, unfulfilled, empty and discouraged? Why can't these people be happy?

The answer is deceptively simple. No one has ever told them how to achieve happiness.

What's Your Concept?

Most human beings have little difficulty conjuring up their own purple-hued vision of the ultimate in human existence - very often a pleasing combination of wealth, status and power, with freedom from frustration, both mentally and sexually. If this vaguely fits your concept of happiness, you really ought to consider whether or not this "vision of Valhalla" is a truly worthwhile goal.

One way to find out is to examine the lives of men who have actually lived under such conditions - and to see where it got them. One of the best examples historically is King Solomon, a real-life figure widely noted throughout the ancient world for his fantastic wealth and wisdom.

Solomon had everything going for him. His father, King David, had at great effort and cost subdued the worst of the neighboring war-hungry tribes and had established a measure of peace in the Kingdom of Israel. After David's death, Solomon stepped into a situation few men have ever had the opportunity to experience - limitless wealth at his personal disposal, a conditional promise of blessings from God and the gift of unparalleled wisdom, also given by God. Gossip undoubtedly circulated far and wide in that ancient world about Solomon's fantastic kingdom.

Foreign royalty paid him state visits to see if what they heard was really true.

It was. What they found in the City of David only served to reinforce the Solomonic legend, even though the truth needed no embellishment. According to the Biblical record published in Second Chronicles, chapters six through nine, Solomon possessed enough wealth and power to luxuriate in a life-style making notorious penthouse-dwellers of today seem poverty-stricken by comparison.

A Catalog of Wealth

On a yearly basis, Solomon received 666 talents of gold , or about 960,000 ounces . That amounts to something like $33,600,000 in gold per year at the old rate of $35 per ounce {$1,248,000,000 per year presuming a gold value of $1300 per ounce}.

There are … individuals today whose yearly assets … exceed that figure on paper, but this was the real thing - solid gold. It was reputedly so common, in fact, that Solomon didn't bother to buy certain items for himself. He had them made from his gold. His throne was made of imported ivory overlaid with gold. None of his drinking vessels were made of silver. It was simply too common, assertedly as common as ordinary rock (I Kings 10:27).

Solomon imported finery from all parts of the world. His navy reported to him each year , bringing him more gold, silver, ivory and rare animals . In a triumph of understatement, I Kings 10:23 says that Solomon exceeded all the kings of the earth in riches and in wisdom. State visits involved extravagant exchanges of gifts. When the famous Queen of Sheba for instance, came to investigate the fabulous rumors she had heard about Solomon, she brought along 120 talents of gold, a "very great store" of spices and precious stones to boot. Nearby friendly King Hiram, who lived on the Mediterranean coast, used his ships to bring Solomon gold from Ophir, as well as large amounts of rare wood and precious stones.

However, money really wasn't everything. The Bible says that Solomon loved "many strange women" (I Kings 11:1). That is another magnificent understatement. Solomon kept seven hundred bona-fide wives plus three hundred concubines. To impress these wives, he commanded a personal army of charioteers - 1,400 chariots, to be exact, and twelve thousand horsemen . He even built special cities for these men, and imported their horses from Egypt. To keep his wives happy, he also ordered the best of imported fabrics (I Kings 10:28- 29).

But Was He Happy?

In addition, Solomon, being king and all-powerful, could of course do anything he desired - which is precisely what he set about to do. Later on, he wrote a book about his exploits called Ecclesiastes.

In this book, Solomon relates how he experimented with nearly everything under the sun to see what might make him happy. Nonstop entertainment soon grew tiresome. "But I found that this, too, was futile. For it is silly to be laughing all the time; what good does it do?" (Eccl. 2:2, The Living Bible.) He mentions taking up drinking to see if happiness could be found in a bottle. Happiness wasn't, but morning-after headaches probably were. He constructed monuments to himself in the form of immense and beautiful public works. They were impressive and undoubtedly provided a great ego-trip, but they seem to have made him no happier. He built elaborate houses for himself and constructed temples for the gods of his favorite pagan wives. He raised vineyards and conducted experiments in his botanical gardens on all kinds of rare trees and plants. He constructed waterworks to irrigate the nearby arid land. Most of this is described in Ecclesiastes, chapter two.

He stated matter of factly, "I became greater than any of the kings in Jerusalem before me, and with it all I remained clear-eyed, so that I could evaluate all these things". This, admittedly, sounds like shades of Muhammad Ali, the boastful American heavyweight boxer, but it was the literal truth. He also confessed that "anything I wanted, I took, and did not restrain myself from any joy" (Eccl. 2:9-10, The Living Bible).

In short, Solomon had fame, money, and wisdom - every physical blessing there was to have. He tried everything there was to try - at least, all he could think of - and he had whatever he wanted whenever he wanted it. It was all paid for. He lacked absolutely nothing in the way of human comfort.

Unfortunately, Solomon was miserable. He admitted it himself. "So now I hate life because it is all so irrational; all is foolishness, chasing the wind" (Eccl. 2:17, The Living Bible).

Why on earth would a man who had everything, including an unrestricted and enormously varied sex life, be so fed up with living that he felt like committing suicide?

The truth is that Solomon knew what would have made him happy - but he ignored it. Had he paid more attention to it, he could have lived a life more like the happier, fulfilled and rewarding existence of another man who lived almost a thousand years later.

From Persecutor to Persecuted

This man seemed to have every right to be miserable. He was Jewish and a member of the sect of the Pharisees. He hated the new sect which was called "Christian" after a certain Jesus Christ who had been publicly executed, but who the Christians claimed was still alive. He considered them an annoying threat to the Jewish religious establishment in which he held a high position. He persecuted the Christians with a vigor that astounded the liberal Romans in charge of that part of the Empire.

This man was forced to undergo conversion to the very "sect" which he had been so avidly persecuting. His former compatriots probably considered him slightly insane to take such a flip-flop in his thinking. The man's name, of course, was Paul. He later became an apostle and one of the chief figures in the development of the New Testament church.

Far from having the magnificent wealth which Solomon had enjoyed, Paul was forced by circumstance to fall back on his childhood training of tentmaking in order to support himself as he ministered to the Churches of God located around the Mediterranean Sea. In addition, he had to do much of his traveling on foot, or by ship. Devastating storms were common occurrences. Then, too, he was under constant danger from those intent upon persecuting the Church as he had once done himself. He didn't always escape their wrath.

He catalogued his "misadventures" in the ministry in one of his published letters to the church located in the Greek city of Corinth:

"Five different times the Jews gave me their terrible thirty nine lashes. Three times I was beaten with rods. Once I was stoned. Three times I was shipwrecked. Once I was in the open sea all night and the whole next day. I have traveled many weary miles and have been often in great danger from flooded rivers, and from robbers, and from my own people, the Jews, as well as from the hands of the Gentiles. I have faced grave dangers from mobs in the cities and from death in the deserts and in the stormy seas and from men who claim to be brothers in Christ but are not. I have lived with weariness and pain and sleepless nights. Often I have been hungry and thirsty and have gone without food; often I have shivered with cold, without enough clothing to keep me warm.

"Then, besides all this, I have the constant worry of how the churches are getting along" (The Living Bible, II Cor. 11:24-28).
That is quite a list of adventures, enough to make men of lesser fortitude to opt for a safe, comfortable office job. But external problems were not all Paul endured. He also had what he called a "thorn in the flesh", possibly a health problem, although he doesn't refer to it specifically by name (II Cor. 12:7). He does imply, that his eyes gave him problems (Gal. 4:15).

In addition, he just wasn't very impressive in person. He says little about this fact, but does mention that others had tried to denigrate him in the sight of his congregation by rather nastily alluding to the fact that he was powerful enough in his letters, but that his bodily presence was weak and his speech contemptible (II Cor. 10:10).

Yet Paul Was Happy

By now you can probably sense the obvious lesson about to hit you between the eyes: Happiness doesn't necessarily come from wealth, position, sexual freedom, or unlimited power and status. A man enduring the worst of living conditions, like Paul, can be happy in spite of the way things look or feel. " . . . For I have learned, in whatsoever state I am, therewith to be content," said Paul in Philippians 4: 11. "I know now how to live when things are difficult and I know how to live when things are prosperous. In general and in particular I have learned the secret of facing either plenty or poverty" (Philippians 4:12, Phillips translation).

What was his secret? What did Paul know that Solomon didn't?

The answer is: NOTHING.

Solomon knew the same basic formula for happy living that Paul preached, but the fact that he ignored it literally ruined his life. As a bitter old man looking backward on years, Solomon advised younger men, made: "Remember now thy Creator in the days of thy youth , while the, evil days come not, nor the years draw nigh, when thou shalt say, I have no pleasure in them ... . Let us hear the conclusion of the whole matter: Fear God, and keep his commandments: refers to as · for this is the whole duty of man" (Eccl . 12:1,13).

"Fear God and keep his commandments." That was the one thing though, which could have made Solomon happy - which would have made his fabulous wealth, not at all wrong in itself, a blessing rather than a frustration. And, obedience to the laws of God was the one ingredient in Paul's life which enabled him to keep going - even to be happy - in spite of all obstacles in his path.

And these same principles, if you obey them, can make you happy--no matter what your situation in life if YOU choose not to ignore them.

But Are They Relevant Today?

"All right," you say, "but we are all living in the twentieth century, not two thousand years ago in a Middle Eastern kingdom noted for its mystical adherents and richly embellished history. How would following an ancient code like the Ten Commandments help anyone living in the city ghetto, or playing the freeway game each day, or struggling with unpaid bills, striving to patch up marital spats, worrying over visits to the hospital, breathing the polluted air? "Isn't telling everyone to do so more than just a little absurd, a gross over-simplification as a solution to complicated human problems?

Not really. The Ten Commandments are timeless and apply no matter which century you happen to have been born into. For instance, the seventh commandment says, in what sounds to many like foreboding tones, "Thou shalt not commit adultery". In other words, "Don't cheat on your wife or husband. It'll make you both unhappy".

It goes without saying that all of mankind is not now obeying God - and probably won't unless forced to. But think, for a moment, of the fantastic results which would occur if everyone on earth were to obey just that one commandment. No more broken homes. No more agonizing heartbreak which cannot be measured statistically. No more wretched childhoods spent first with one parent, then with the other, always with the tension and insecurity which accompanies such a childhood situation, and which very often produces deep problems in the adult years. If everyone were striving to obey JUST this ONE commandment, the very marriage covenant would not be entered into so blithely. Young couples would take marriage much more seriously if they realized they were marrying for life, and not simply until the next attractive body comes around. In short, obedience to that one commandment could save mankind from a whole host of premarital and marital problems, heartaches and tragedies.

But that is only one commandment out of ten, only one example of why Solomon's advice to "fear God and keep his commandments" is an open invitation to a happier, fuller, more satisfying life - the kind of life God wants every human being to experience.

If you would like to have more information about the Ten Commandments , explaining how all of them are applicable to life in today's world, check out our free online book, available atwww.ccog.org, titled: 'The Ten Commandments: The Decalogue, Christianity, and the Beast.'

Youth & Singles: Q&A

Q. So many guys today seem to think dating and sexual intercourse automatically go together. I haven't given in to my boyfriend yet, but I'm feeling the pressure and I don't want to lose him. Can you help me?

A. God's law forbids premarital sex (Exodus 20:14, 1 Corinthians 6:8). Having sex before marriage is a grave mistake many regret later in life.

Look at this letter, for example:

> "I always thought of myself as a nice girl because I wouldn't go 'all the way'. With every new boyfriend, necking became just the thing to do. But also with each it became less exciting …
>
> "About four years ago after losing my virginity, I met the man who would become my husband. I cannot put into words how much I love this man. However, there is a major problem. Because of my previous sexual experience, my senses are deadened. How I wish I could go back and erase all the relationships I had with other men. What a true blessing it must be to have a wonderful sexual life with your mate!"

The young woman who wrote the letter above points out just one sad result of premarital sexual experimentation. There are many others, including unwanted pregnancy, abortion, and a vast array of sexually transmissible diseases.

If the young man you are dating doesn't respect you enough not to stay with you unless you will engage in premarital sex, how much do you think he really cares about you?

You will have to decide what you value more - the temporary (and it tends to be just that, despite promises of permanency) attention of a guy or your chance for personal happiness for many years to come. Men will have to decide whether to indulge in temporary physical pleasure now or to buck the crowd and wait to enjoy sex with that one special woman in a loving marriage, as God intended. Christians know what God teaches on this.

Choose God's way of life and you will not regret it!

Q. If a guy really is sweet to me, doesn't that mean he is committed and we should have sex even if we are not married?

A. No.

Notice something that happened to a teenage female who contacted the old Worldwide Church of God:

> "I am 14 years old and I have had sex twice. After reading the article signed: 'Learning From My Mistakes'' it made me realize how wrong I was. It even brought tears to my eyes. I thought or made myself think that it was all right to have sex as long as you like the boy you're with. But now I know how wrong I was. The guys I was with were very sweet to me only before we ever did anything. Now we don't even talk to each other. The day after it happened, they called me all the names in the book--at the time it really hurt. NOW it haunts me day and night. I know there are a lot of teens out there that know what I'm talking about. I have never told my parents about this; for all they know I'm a sweet little innocent angel sitting on top of the world and it hurts to think that I let them down." This sad little girl ended her letter with a request for the brochure "Sexually Transmissible Diseases" and the book "The Missing Dimension in Sex … "

Throughout history, guys have used similar techniques, and countless females have fallen for the temporary attention. Do not believe the lie—if a man will not marry you first, you never should have sex with him.

Q. Others in the Church have ignored what it recommended related to dating and marriage, and gotten married. Why shouldn't I do that?

A. Most who ignore God's principles relating to dating and marriage, will have regrets—major regrets.

Many will get divorced. Many will have numerous problems and will one day wish that they did things God's way.

Consider:

> 19 Do not fret because of evildoers, Nor be envious of the wicked; 20 For there will be no prospect for the evil man; The lamp of the wicked will be put out. (Proverbs 24:19-20)

It really does not end up better for people who will not trust God.

The Apostle John wrote:

> 19 We love Him because He first loved us. (1 John 4:19)

We are able to respond to God because He loved us first. That sets the major pattern for all human relationships, including male-female interaction.

More on the dating related questions can be found in our free online book, available at www.ccog.org, titled: "Dating: A Key to Success in Marriage, a practical dating guide for Christians'.

We are open to covering other questions that are not in our booklet as well. If you have appropriate questions that you would like answered here, you can send them to the Continuing Church of God at the address shown in the front of this magazine or send an email for consideration.

More FREE *Continuing Church of God* Books and Booklets
at www.ccog.org/books

Proof Jesus is the Messiah

The Decalogue, Christianity, and the Beast

Should You Keep God's Holy Days or Demonic Holidays?

Where Is The True Christian Church Today?